VITAL 3
Effective Leadership in Schools

Book 2

Innovation ...

and the future challenges of effective leadership

Tony Swainston

Published by Network Educational Press Ltd
PO Box 635
Stafford
ST16 1BF

First published 2005
© Tony Swainston 2005

ISBN 1 85539 124 4

Project editor: Anne Oppenheimer
Design and layout: Marc Maynard, Network Educational Press Ltd
Illustrations: Paul Keen and Tony Swainston

Printed in Great Britain by
MPG Books Ltd, Bodmin, Cornwall

Contents

Book 2: Innovation ... and the future challenges of effective leadership

'Truly effective leaders in the years ahead will have personas determined by strong values and belief in the capacity of individuals to grow. They will have an image of the society in which they would like their organizations and themselves to live.'

Richard Beckhard

Introduction

VITAL 3 Part 2 explores a number of issues in educational leadership that are both challenging and exciting. The significance of innovation in leadership is discussed by the leaders we filmed, and the responses can be studied here in Part 2. All too often we hear about innovation in education, and to a certain extent people may almost become weary with the idea, believing that a period of consolidation is what is most needed. This feeling I would sympathize with – if 'innovation' had no impact on building systemic change that is beneficial for the long term in education. I would also sympathize if innovation got in the way of, or prevented, good practice from continuing and flourishing. However, I believe that innovation is of value – with the proviso that it results in systemic change without getting rid of good practice that exists already. Change is useless, unless it improves things.

Besides, the notion of innovation I am referring to here does not necessarily involve anything that is brand new. Rather, it entails taking ideas that are already out there and making more sense of them in a variety of settings, so that they then benefit many rather than few. Most ideas in education are not new, but taking the best ideas and making use of them is part of innovation. Examples of this that are around at the moment are personalized learning and assessment for learning. Both of these ideas have been around for some time, but many now seem to feel that they can significantly influence learning. It could be argued, therefore, that innovation in respect of these ideas means taking what we know about them and making them available for many people and many schools. This is what Alistair Smith has so successfully done with his work on 'accelerated learning'.

Linked with innovation are the challenges we all face in education, and in particular in leadership within education. We need to look constantly at good practice, to adapt ideas and to learn from each other in order to face the uncertainty of tomorrow with confidence.

In this book I will refer to the work of Jim Collins. His extensive work, which looks at successful leaders who have moved their organizations on from 'being good to being great', is worth consideration in terms of what it can teach us about the leaders we need in our schools, and in all layers of educational leadership, if we are to advance the education system for all our pupils.

In this book, Sections One and Two contain the questions that I asked the leaders who were filmed for VITAL 3.

I hope that you enjoy and find reward in studying Book 2, and that it provides a mechanism for you to reflect by yourself or with colleagues about some of the critical issues impacting on leadership in education today.

Tony Swainston
January 2005

The future

This section concerns the following:

2.1.1   What does the future hold for leadership?
 ▸ The sensitive leader – again demonstrating that the soft things are the hard things

2.1.2   Creating the future
 ▸ Leaders who determine the shape of education for the future

2.1.3   Living the dream
 ▸ Leaders can still be dreamers too!

2.1.4   Important skills of the future
 ▸ What should education be all about?

2.1.5   The UNESCO four fundamentals
 ▸ The pillars of learning

2.1.6   Finally, the section looks at the responses of the leaders to the questions on the future which include:

Supplementary DVD with background information
a)   What do you see as the leadership challenges for schools in the immediate future?
b)   What innovations do you feel will impact most on changing people's views on leadership in the future?

2.1.1 What does the future hold for leadership?

What appears to be certain is that no matter how leadership ideas might change, the role of the leader in the future of schools will remain significant. The question is, what the role will look like? A number of people now believe that one of the chief roles of the headteacher will be as a supporter and developer of people in the school, working at harnessing and releasing the energy of people to serve the overall vision of the school. The successful headteacher will also be conscious of the development of teachers and all staff in a broad sense, being sensitive and aware of their physical and mental health. This is something that is high on the present agenda, with the reform of the workforce and the attention being given to the recruitment and retention of teachers in particular. Blanchard (in Hesselbein et al. 1996) expresses this as follows:

'To help people win, the leader of the future must be able to manage energy and change people's physical state of being. Setting the vision will focus people's attention and provide direction. Once the vision is set and people are committed to it, the role of the leader is to turn his or her attention to physiology – how people are acting and performing within the organization – and to align their performance with the vision. Here is where the leader of the future will excel as a cheerleader, supporter, and encourager rather than as a judge, critic or evaluator. Helping people align their behaviour with the organization's vision will solidify the attaining of desired goals and move energy in the desired direction. This results in an ultimate organization where people not only know where they are headed but are empowered to get there.'

At the same time many of the qualities of effective leaders of the past will remain the same for future leaders. So, for example, Kanter (in Hesselbein et al. 1996) describes certain ways in which the characteristics of the leader of tomorrow will be similar to those of the past:

'Thus in most important ways, leaders of the future will need the traits and capabilities of leaders throughout history: an eye for change and a steadying hand to provide both vision and reassurance that change can be mastered, a voice that articulates the will of the group and shapes it to constructive ends, and an ability to inspire by force of personality while making others feel empowered to increase and use their abilities.'

There is a general belief now that leaders of the future will have to be outward-looking, prepared to network and seek expertise from outside their own schools. In fact, schools of the future may not look like schools of the past. Walls will be – both metaphorically and in reality at times – broken down, and bridges built, with educational boundaries becoming blurred. Whom the school serves in terms of its clients will be more complex, with the school itself often acting as a broker for the education of pupils. Many writers have said that schools and other formal organizations for learning will just be seen as one element of learning in the future. The following view of leaders in general is very pertinent to schools:

> 'Leaders of the future can no longer afford to maintain insularity. It is simply not an option in an increasingly borderless world of boundaryless organizations driven by "customer power": the fact is that people can increasingly bypass local monopolies or protected local suppliers and shop the world for the best goods and services. In short, leaders of the past often erected walls. Now they must destroy those walls and replace them with bridges.' (Kanter in Hesselbein et al. 1996)

2.1.2 Creating the future

Whatever the future brings, the guiding principles of strong moral purpose and vision will continue to be important. A belief in people and what they can achieve, together with the desire to live out or model the kind of approach to life that they want from others, is all part of the leader's role. All the leaders in the present work express this in a variety of ways. Beckhard (in Hesselbein et al. 1996) writes:

> 'Truly effective leaders in the years ahead will have personas determined by strong values and belief in the capacity of individuals to grow. They will have an image of the society in which they would like their organizations and themselves to live. They will be visionary, they will believe strongly that they can and should be shaping the future, and they will act on those beliefs through their personal behaviour.'

Leaders will have to be adventurous, to seize opportunities and to be prepared to model what the future is to be, rather than accepting what comes along. The government is saying that it wants to give greater ownership to schools. If this is the case, the onus on leaders to be creative and form their own futures is perhaps more important than ever before. Ulrich (in Hesselbein et al. 1996) says:

> *Future leaders will need to be pioneers who take risks, create new paths, shape new approaches to old problems, and have strong values and beliefs that drive their actions.*

2.1.3 Living the dream

Having a dream about the future is part of the vision and optimism of the headteachers filmed for VITAL 3. Living the dream, living the vision and living the story will be important for leaders of the future – as indeed it is today. Along with this, leaders of the future must have personal credibility which involves having the 'personal habits, values, traits and competencies to engender trust and commitment from those who take their direction' (Ulrich in Hesselbein et al. 1996). Mahatma Gandhi is one of the people mentioned by those filmed for VITAL 3 as a leader that they admire, and Gandhi, of course, was full of personal credibility. Gandhi claimed:

> *My life is its own message. You must watch my life, how I live, eat, sit, talk, behave in general. The sum total of all those is my religion.*

Crucially the leader of the future will not have all the answers – did they ever? Asking the right questions, motivating, empowering and distributing leadership, will all be important. The leaders of the past may have been people who told others what to do, but the leaders of the future will grow leaders around them, constantly asking questions to fully involve others in the organization, to seek out their views on complex issues, and to show that they have the desire to constantly learn. Goldsmith (in Hesselbein et al. 1996) says:

> 'The leader of the past was a person who knew how to tell. The leader of the future will be a person who knows how to ask. The effective leader of the future will consistently and efficiently ask, learn, follow up, and grow. The leader who cannot keep learning and growing will soon become obsolete in tomorrow's ever-changing world.'

Goldsmith goes on to emphasize the importance of asking questions as a way for leaders to present themselves as role models with humility and a desire to learn:

> 'Aside from the obvious benefit of gaining new ideas and insights, asking by top leaders has a secondary benefit that may be even more important. The leader who asks is providing a role model. Sincere asking demonstrates a willingness to learn, a desire to serve, and a humility that can be an inspiration for the entire organization.'

Writers such as Watkins et al. (1996) have said that the knowledge base is doubling every four years. This is an example of how the world that young people will be growing up in is so radically changing. In this changing world we need to be constantly asking the fundamental question about the key purpose of education. This is, of course, an ongoing debate that may never reveal a complete answer, but this doesn't mean that the question should no longer be asked, nor the debate continue. With family structures changing, people living longer, and 'jobs for life' no longer being the case, in the future schools will need to constantly reflect o*n their key role in society.

> 'In such turbulent times the inescapable question is, "What should education be for? What are its essential purposes?"' (MacBeath and Mortimore 2001)

This is touched on, on the following page.

2.1.4 Important skills of the future

Traditional perspectives on the nature of education, involving key components providing literacy, numeracy and technological competence, may remain, but schools will need to provide far more if pupils are to be able to face the future with confidence. As MacBeath and Mortimore suggest, the following skills will be equally important.

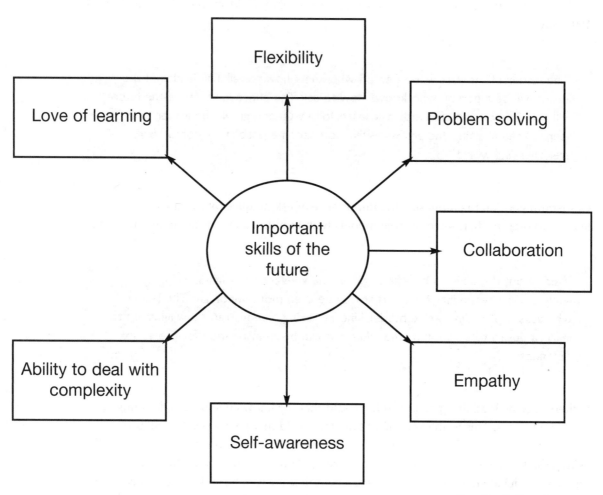

Diagram by Tony Swainston

Leaders in schools will be crucially important in terms of ensuring that the nurturing of the skills shown above is something that is part of their school. There is now a greater concentration on, and debate around, emotional intelligence, and many of these skills fall into this general description. Without the capacity to constantly learn in an ever-changing world, the future options of young people will be dramatically reduced.

2.1.5 The UNESCO four fundamentals

In 1996 UNESCO identified 'four fundamental types of learning which, throughout a person's life, will, in a way, be the pillars of knowledge'. It is worth looking at these again here and considering here how they should form part of the thinking of leaders in schools, so as to ensure that those leaders are serving the needs of their pupils.

Four pillars of learning (based on UNESCO 1996)

LEARNING TO BE

Developing a greater autonomy, judgement and personal responsibility, through attention to all aspects of a person's potential.

LEARNING TO LIVE TOGETHER

Developing understanding of others and appreciation of independence, to participate and cooperate with others

LEARNING TO KNOW	LEARNING TO DO
Acquiring a broad general knowledge, the instruments of understanding, and learning to learn	The competence to deal with many situations and to act creatively on one's environment

Diagram by Tony Swainston

2.1.6 The future – what the leaders filmed for VITAL 3 say

Derek echoes the views expressed above, that the key purpose of schools in future may well be very different from what it is today. He says that schools will no longer be the centre of learning but rather will operate as brokers and experts in learning. He adds that *'The nature of schooling and education is changing.'*

Susan expresses one of the frustrations that many leaders in schools face. She says that *'... one of the greatest challenges is the number of initiatives flooding into schools. Most of it is excellent, but...'* The 'but' is that the quantity of initiatives can sometimes feel overwhelming for some.

Janet talks about the need to *'restore the balanced curriculum'*, while Phil expresses a similar concern about *'how you can restore creativity into the heart of schools'*. Mike adds *'I think perhaps the greatest influence on changing people's views of leadership is refocusing on the holistic education of young people'* rather than primarily on exams. Eddie sees the future as being one where we may be able to move from '*an outcomes-driven culture to a learning-driven, supportive culture*'.

Theresa, like many leaders, has concerns about the outcome-measures culture and believes that there should now be an acknowledgement of *'the distinctive nature of each school'*. Mike feels that managing an ageing workforce will be a challenge, together with the reform of the workforce. He adds that *'it will take a mind-shift in how we manage learning for young people'*.

Anne says that there are some *'immediate, nitty-gritty problems'* and that these can get in the way of the big ideas. David expresses how the litigious society is impacting on headship, and can, as he feels, put some people off becoming heads. Iain concurs with this and feels that encouraging and motivating people to become headteachers is a challenge, even though he says the rewards are great.

Chris feels that *'the biggest challenge is about partnerships'* and about offering more entitlement to both pupils and staff, while Kay shares the views of many writers that how to maintain positive relationships at all times is a real challenge in leadership. Positive relationships bring enjoyment, and Theresa says, *'Enjoyment is a huge motivator. Motivation, I think, is something we need to get back to talking about.'* Susan feels that a real challenge is '*to be realistic about what you can achieve as a headteacher*'.

Helen feels that the future will involve the fact that *'people are going to be involved in leadership from an earlier stage'*, and Janet talks about learning from networking and observing others. She says, *'I think the way we learn best is by watching and seeing what is good in other schools.'*

'Future leaders will need to be pioneers who take risks, create new paths, shape new approaches to old problems, and have strong values and beliefs that drive their actions.'

Dave Ulrich

Aspects of leadership

This section concerns the following:

2.2.1 The leadership constellation

> ▸ Sustaining leadership

2.2.2 The varied characteristics of leadership

> ▸ The many contradictions that need to be managed

2.2.3 Communication

> ▸ Without communication, a leader cannot lead.

2.2.4 Finally, the section looks at the leaders' responses to questions about aspects of leadership, which include:

Questions on aspects of leadership

a) To what extent does leadership depend on charisma?
b) Is confidence a vital ingredient in leadership?
c) To what extent does leadership involve acting? Is this something that you consciously do?
d) Who can a leader turn to when there is concern about what direction to take at a critical point of decision?
e) To what extent is leadership about imagination, innovation and change? Is there an example in your leadership that could illustrate this?

2.2.1 The leadership constellation

A great deal of discussion concerning the agenda for leadership in the future has so far been, and will continue to be, around the issue of managing change. People feel wary of change, as they sense moving from established and familiar circumstances into the relative unknown. However, schools will need to reflect, adapt and change to the new circumstances that are continually happening in our society and the shifting way we view the whole business of what schools are intended to do, as mentioned earlier. Writers like Michael Fullan have said that when change is mentioned people can experience sensations of fear, anxiety, loss, danger, and panic. On the other hand, they may also think of positive aspects to change, illustrated by words such as 'exhilaration', 'risk-taking', 'excitement', 'improvements', and 'energizing'. Fullan (2001) says:

> *For better or worse, change arouses emotions, and when emotions intensify, leadership is key.*

Change is inevitable, and Heifetz (quoted in Fullan) talks about leaders 'mobilizing people to tackle tough problems'. Fullan goes on to say that leadership is not mobilizing others to solve problems we already know how to solve, but helping them to confront problems that have never yet been successfully addressed. These truly are the tough problems.

But in order for change to take place, Fullan says that there must be a culture of change. This does not involve taking on board every innovation that comes along, but it does mean 'producing the capacity to seek, critically assess, and selectively incorporate new ideas and practices – all the time, inside the organization as well as outside it'. Leadership, and certainly leadership that invites change, Fullan adds, also crucially involves the following 'leadership constellation':

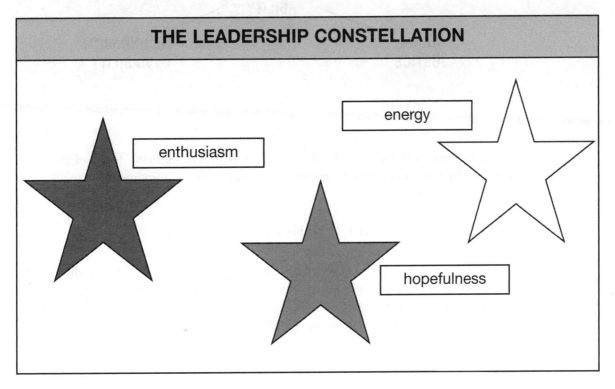

Diagram by Tony Swainston

Leadership of change requires significant energy and drive, coupled with enthusiasm for the challenge and that deep-seated sense of hopefulness that permeates all great leaders. A leader needs energy, particularly in starting up or taking over an organization. Without this the daily battle to strive for the best and to inspire those around you that need to be lifted may prove to be all too much. Schein (in Hesselbein et al. 1996)says:

'At the early stages of organizational creation, a unique leadership function is to supply the energy needed to get the organization off the ground. Much is said about the vision of entrepreneurs, but not enough is said about the incredible energy they display as they try one approach after another, facing repeated failures, in their efforts to start an enterprise.'

Fullan adds to this that it is important for sustainability that there should be the trinity of *environmental soundness*, *social justice* and *economic viability*.

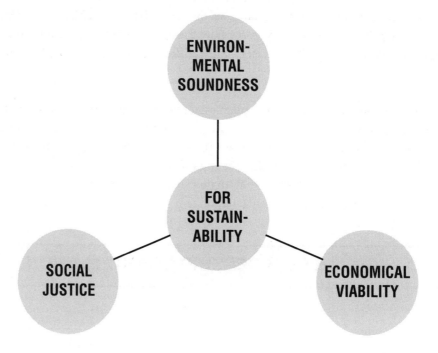

This is a rich mix of the social/ethical perspective with the pragmatic aspect of the economy which need to operate together within the natural environment.

2.2.2 The varied characteristics of leadership

Successful leadership requires many personal characteristics. Handy (in Hesselbein et al. 1996) says that 'few people do it successfully, because it demands an unusual combination of attributes'. Some of these seem like opposites or paradoxes. The diagram opposite represents examples given by Handy.

A belief in oneself	**A decent doubt**
The only thing that gives an individual the self-confidence to step into the unknown and to persuade others to go where no one has gone before.	The humility to accept that one can be wrong on occasion, that others have ideas, that listening is as important as talking.
A passion for the job	**An awareness of other worlds**
This provides the energy and focus that drive the organization and that act as an example to others.	Focus can turn to a blinkered view of the world, therefore it is important to think outside the box. Great leaders find time to read, to meet people beyond their own circle, to go to the theatre or see films, to walk in other worlds.
A love of people	**A capacity for aloneness**
Those who find individuals a pain may be respected or feared, but they will not be willingly followed.	Leaders have to be out front. Few will thank the leader when things go right, but many will blame the leader if things go wrong. Great leaders have to walk alone from time to time. They also have to live vicariously, deriving their satisfaction from the successes of others and giving to others the recognition that they themselves are often denied.

It cannot be easy to successfully manage these very different characteristics, and Handy says: 'Living with these paradoxes requires great strength of character. It also requires a belief in what one is doing.'

Writers including Ulrich (in Hesselbein et al. 1996) have added to the debate about the complex and paradoxical nature of leadership in that:

▶ it is an art and a science

▶ it involves change and stability

▶ it draws on personal attributes and requires interpersonal relationships

▶ it sets visions and results in action

▶ it honours the past and exists for the future

▶ it manages things and leads people

▶ it is transformational and transactional

▶ it serves employees and customers

▶ it requires learning and unlearning

▶ it centres on values and it is seen in behaviours.

Ulrich (*ibid.*) says:

> ... *leadership, like the inner workings of a computer, is a complex set of relationships, systems, and processes that few fully master.*

On the other hand, it is comforting for education that Handy also feels that the non-profit arenas of leadership, such as that found in schools, provide great leaders, and that other leaders from the business sector could well benefit from the training given by schools and other non-profit organizations.

As an organization grows and develops, the leader must sustain the momentum. At this stage the successful leaders are the ones who either have enough personal insight to grow with the organization and change their own outlook or, alternatively, 'recognize their limitations and permit other forms of leadership to emerge' (Schein, in Hesselbein 1996).

A lovely definition of an effective leader comes from John W. Work (*ibid.*):

> *They are those individuals who, in their inimitable ways, inspire confidence, understand despair, fight fear, initiate positive and productive actions, light the candles, define the goals, and paint brighter tomorrows.*

Work (in Hesselbein et al. 1996) says something that is consistently spoken about by the leaders filmed for VITAL 3. This is the fact that they all want to make a difference, and becoming the leader through being a headteacher was the way for them of achieving this aim. Work says:

> *Ultimately, true leadership makes a difference in the lives of people.*

Day et al. (2003) talk about the importance of creating trust, building professional communities and developing capacity as key elements required in 'the leaders we need if our schools are to become the high performing systems we all dream about'.

Day et al. say that their own work and other studies of effective leadership and management of highly effective business leaders and headteachers in England and elsewhere confirm a number of things, namely that:

▸ they are person-centred and strongly driven by sets of personal values (religious, spiritual, humanistic)

▸ this creates a 'passionate conviction' to build, implement and continually monitor a vision for excellence in learning and achievement by means of feedback from stakeholders inside and outside the school

▸ skills and behaviours of effective leaders are driven by beliefs and trust in self and others

▸ effective leaders recognize and are skilled in managing tensions and dilemmas within a framework of competing values

- leadership is as much about developing the self alongside high levels of emotional commitment as it is about capacity building in others

- effective leadership requires an intelligent head with an intelligent heart.

A warning about the dangers of achieving high office in leadership has been given by a number of writers. Kakabadse et al. (1998) say, '… as early as 386 BC, Plato initiated one of the first leadership training centres in the world, an institute he called the Academy, in an attempt to create a new type of statesman, a person who would be able to withstand the pressures of office.'

Plato was aware of the 'dark side' of leaders and developed a draconian curriculum to inhibit undesired sentiments and ambition from coming to the fore. Other historical leaders, such as the biblical King Saul, Rome's Caligula and Russia's Ivan the Terrible, and today Iraq's Saddam Hussein and Serbia's Slobodan Milosevic, as well as business leaders who resort to pathological behaviour upon reaching the top, 'provide ample examples of the satanic side of leadership that Plato wanted to guard against. For Plato the possession of a "wisdom", the "one truth" of an "intellectual vision", providing the pathway to effective government as it assists in the appropriate conduct of human affairs, distinguishes leaders from followers' (Kakabadse et al. 1998).

The challenge of leadership is evident when MacBeath (2001) comments that despite all the work done on leadership 'we are still unable to say with confidence how ineffective schools become effective, or indeed to agree on what would constitute an effective school for the third millennium.' All of this is still to be discovered, and leaders of tomorrow have the challenge and opportunity to reveal these things.

Dealing with the complexities of the world requires leaders to generate more and more ideas. Position and personalities will become less important. Sergiovanni (2002) says that in leadership 'three qualities stand out: the capacity to synthesize, to innovate, and to be perceptive'.

Capacity to synthesize	Capacity to innovate	Capacity to be perceptive
Leaders who have mastered the capacity to synthesize are able to sort through and make sense of large amounts of information, identifying what is important and putting this knowledge together to reach powerful, often new, conclusions.	Leaders who have mastered the capacity to innovate are able to combine the elements that are now known in new ways to solve problems.	Leaders who have mastered the capacity to be perceptive have an intuitive knack for identifying what is really important, for understanding what makes a situation run or work in a certain way, and for figuring out what to do about it.

And how about Sergiovanni's analogy between the skills needed to guide a giant amoeba across a street and the nature of leadership? I am sure many experienced leaders will have felt this at times:

'Running a school is like trying to get a giant amoeba to move from one side of the street to another. As the "glob" slips off the kerb onto the street and begins its meandering journey, the job of the leader is to figure out how to keep it together, while trying to move it in the general direction of the other side. This involves pulling here, pushing there, patching holes, supporting thin parts, and breaking up logjams.

The pace is fast and furious as the leader moves first here, then there. Throughout, she or he is never quite sure where the glob will wind up, but never loses sight of the overall goal of getting it to the other side. Mind, heart, and hand become one as the leader "plays" the glob, relying on her or his nose for globbiness, and the ability to discern and anticipate patterns of movement that emerge.'

Leadership can be like guiding a giant glob.

Effective Leadership in Schools

2.2.3 Communication

The leaders in VITAL 3 all agree that communication is both critical and often difficult to achieve successfully. For a headteacher it is important to be able to communicate well, both within the school and also to the broader audience outside the school. This communication may be verbal but also involves the actions the leader takes. To clearly act out what is said is critical in communicating a message that is congruent and therefore is acceptable and has impact.

Warren Bennis, in *On Becoming a Leader* (2003), based his ideas about leadership 'on the assumption that leaders are people who are able to express themselves fully... They also know what they want, why they want it, and how to communicate what they want to others, in order to gain their cooperation and support.'

In terms of verbally communicating messages, a number of leaders, including those filmed here for VITAL 3, say that they are often nervous about this in their early days, but that with experience the task becomes less daunting. Communication, in all its various ways, is an example of a leadership skill that can be significantly developed through experience, reflection and learning.

2.2.4 Aspects of leadership – what the leaders say

To what extent does leadership depend on charisma?

Chris is able to draw on his experience of working in three LEAs and visiting many schools. He says: *'Those of us who have seen highly effective schools know that there are many different types of leader. It's all about how those people create an ethos and a culture which engages and empowers their teams, distributes leadership throughout the teams, and creates a learning culture throughout the organization. From my research the charismatic leaders don't create great institutions. They create good institutions – but for great institutions you need something else, and it's not charisma.'*

David felt that there were certain advantages to a leader possessing charisma, but not in the long term: *'Charisma is very good for short-term effects. For long-term effects on schools charisma is not very helpful, because people become very dependent on charisma.'*

Theresa felt that charisma could play a small part but that this was not sufficient on its own: *'I think it depends to some extent on charisma, but it would be very dangerous if it only depended on charisma.'*

Derek, too, suggested that charisma was not really a major aspect of leadership: *'I think charisma might help, but personally I don't think charisma is the issue to do with leadership.'*

Kay makes the important point that an institution can become too dependent on a charismatic leader. A charismatic leader tends not necessarily to build the capacity for the

---

institution to grow and prosper when they are not there. For this reason Kay says she never wants to be described as charismatic and adds that otherwise, when the head leaves, the whole thing can collapse. Kay feels she wants to develop a school with clear processes and systems so that it doesn't matter if she is there or not.

Mike makes the clear point that *'No one individual should be greater than the institution they serve.'*

Anne says that *'it depends on your definition of charisma'*, and Helen adds that, although she does not believe charisma is essential, it is *'vitally important that you are able to inspire people and carry out the vision you have'*. Phil says he thinks it can help, but that *'if you rely on charisma you might fail'*. He adds that it is the belief systems and other qualities that give leaders their great strength. Iain definitely doesn't believe that charisma is important but rather that self-belief and vision, amongst other qualities, are the important things. Regarding whether charisma matters, Iain adds: *'If it did, I wouldn't be a headteacher.'*

Eddie and Janet agree that it is a range of other leadership qualities that are important, such as presence, enthusiasm, commitment and the ability to inspire people.

Is confidence a vital ingredient in leadership?

All the leaders filmed felt that, unlike charisma, confidence was important. For example, David says: *'I think confidence is top of the list.'*

Chris agrees with the importance of confidence and adds: *'I don't think you can do this job, because it is so complex, without being confident, having high self-esteem … most importantly having high expectations and valuing the people who work in your organization.'*

Anne says: *'People have to have confidence in you.'*

There is a sense from some of the leaders, though, that confidence mustn't then appear as arrogance or dogmatism (Theresa) and the belief that the leader knows all the answers and can do everything on their own. Susan, for example, says, *'… but I don't think that confidence needs to all come from you.'* Phil adds to the warning about confidence, saying: *'I think confidence is essential. But I've often met people who are overconfident. There is a thin divide between arrogance and confidence.'* Ian captures the essence of this when he says that confidence is important, *'but you must have humility.'*

Derek develops the idea that confidence *'could include the confidence to know that you don't necessarily know the answer'*. He adds that *'great leaders are prepared to take risks'* and this is perhaps one of the biggest aspects of confidence. Janet supports this and says, *'… if we always do what we've always done, we always get what we've always got.'*

Another important feature of confidence is defined by Mike, who says: *'If you are in any doubt about your own confidence and your own abilities, then the chances are you are not going to listen to criticisms when you need them.'*

All leaders need to listen to others, and to have the confidence to do this, even when what they hear is perhaps not immediately appealing.

To what extent does leadership involve acting? Is this something that you consciously do?

The concept of acting can be challenging for some because it conjures up the notion of insincerity. Clearly everyone would agree that insincerity in leadership is not acceptable, but the leaders filmed did give some varied and interesting views on where acting might be appropriate in certain situations.

Derek clearly states the need for sincerity. He says, *'I think we go into a certain role,'* but adds that this may not be acting and that it is important that *'whatever you are doing, integrity shines through.'* Phil supports this when he says, *'It must be based on substance.'* Susan expresses this by saying, *'What you see is what you get,'* and Janet gives a similar comment to this.

Chris, Janet and Kay definitely feel that leadership does not involve acting. On the other hand, Helen says that she thinks *'every teacher is an actor really'* and that in leadership there are times when you need to act as well. (The concept of acting in teaching is discussed in VITAL 1 and 2). David takes this one step further and says, *'I'm conscious I do it all the time. I do it for effect.'*

Anne talks about the difference between her roles as *'Anne Clarke the private person and Anne Clarke the headteacher'*, but she is careful to point out that this is not a matter of acting so much as the different approaches she adopts at home and at school.

Eddie says about acting that *'it is important for self-preservation at times'*, and Theresa says that *'it is not something I consciously do, but I think it's there'*. Phil uses an actor's language when he says that *'you've got to be able to judge the audience'*. Speaking to groups when there has been a tragedy (as talked about by one of the leaders) may require a high degree of acting if it is felt that it is more appropriate to hide your instinctive feelings at that moment.

Who can a leader turn to when there is concern about the direction to take at a critical decision?

Some people comment that the job of being a headteacher can be a lonely one. Some of the leaders we filmed agree that it can be, but the majority view seemed to be that there are plenty of people you can turn to. These include:

▸ family

▸ governors

▸ staff

▸ those whom the decision will affect

▸ leadership group

▸ senior team

▸ LEA

▸ parents

▸ 'coach'.

To what extent is leadership about imagination, innovation and change? Is there an example in your leadership that could illustrate this?

Eddie says that in leadership he feels there is no rulebook and therefore imagination is essential. Mike says that *'imagination, innovation and creativity are central parts of what I would perceive to be high quality leadership.'*

Imagination is needed because in education there is constant change. Anne says, *'I love change.'* Chris adds that in his view some change can happen gradually. He says *'I do believe leadership is about passion and creativity and imagination and ideas, but that doesn't necessarily mean it's about revolution.'*

However, as Ian and Janet explain, sometimes imagination, innovation and change are needed to challenge the system and look for new ways of doing things.

'The leader of the past was a person who knew how to tell.

The leader of the future will be a person who knows how to ask.

The effective leader of the future will consistently and efficiently ask, learn, follow-up, and grow.

The leader who cannot keep learning and growing will soon become obsolete in tomorrow's ever-changing world.'

Marshall Goldsmith

Further thoughts on leadership

This section concerns the following:

2.3.1 Don't aim for a work–life balance!

▸ It is all life.

2.3.2 What reform?

▸ Leadership leading the revolution.

2.3.3 Creativity – what is it all about?

▸ It's needed for advancement.

2.3.4 Capacity – can we fill it?

▸ How full can we become?

2.3.1 Don't aim for a work–life balance!

A lot of attention is now being paid to what is called the 'work–life balance'. Perhaps the issue is not to get the work–life balance right, because this implies a division that can only create friction between the two, with competing demands. Rather it could be argued that it is the role of the leader to guide those in the school (through developing the correct atmosphere and ethos within the school) into a position where there is a 'life' that combines both work life and home life. This is preferable to the concept of a 'work–life balance' – which implies that work is on one side, trying to turn us in one direction, in conflict with our life, which is trying to turn us in the opposite direction. In an ideal situation both aspects together provide the rewards that combine to produce life-fulfilment. There should be no visible seam, in an ideal world.

There is something deeply fundamental about this, in the sense that it fundamentally alters the way we view our lives. It moves us away from the old notion that we work simply to provide for the life we really want to be living. 'Life' is all that we do, and the fulfilment and nourishment of the work we do should enrich the life we live. That is what a number of people are fortunate enough to experience already in the work they do. The aim of the leader should be for this to apply to everyone, and it is important to change our thinking from 'work–life balance' to simply 'life-balance' because the message this sends out is very powerful: – that life is an indivisible whole.

2.3.2 What reform?

As has been emphasized throughout this book, schools are part of the change mechanism in society – they need to respond to the external change influencing them, but they also need to lead the change to drive the agenda for tomorrow. Like most organizations, schools have to respond to this within the confines of the established roles and the custom and practice that have developed. People can find change difficult if they think that they themselves have to change. The requirement is to be able to sincerely comfort and reassure people that it not them as individuals that need to change, but that part of the work that they will be doing will change, and for the better, in such a way that their lives will be improved. With workforce reform now high on the agenda, school leaders have an important role to carry out in bringing about the changes that should benefit the profession as a whole. William Bridges (in Hesselbein et al. 1996) describes why this can be difficult to carry out in any organization. He says:

'Jobs make it hard for an organization to respond to change effectively. The market changes, but people keep doing their job instead of shifting their attention to whatever most needs to be done.'

Without the necessary changes, however, any organization can find itself left behind, and again, Bridges warns that 'in a rapidly changing environment … a company can go bankrupt while all its employees are doing their job perfectly'. This echoes the idea of the difference between management and leadership expressed by many, including Covey (in Hesselbein et al. 1996). (See Book 3 page 15.) Efficiency is no good, unless what is done is done effectively.

2.3.3 Creativity – what is it all about?

One of the great challenges for schools now is to find creative solutions to the never-ending stream of demands and difficult problems that they encounter. Schools are being asked to be individual and creative within the framework of a centrally driven educational agenda. The effective leaders of tomorrow will be those people who can manage these seemingly paradoxical demands within the particular circumstances in which their schools operate. There is an abundance of information that potentially can bring knowledge and growth. How schools manage this will be critical for their future advancement, and the methods of successfully accomplishing this may not be entirely obvious. Creativity, therefore, will be essential if the teaching and learning on offer in schools is to match the needs of the pupils.

> 'In a knowledge economy more people need to be creative and this will in itself require new approaches to teaching.' (Hargreaves 2003)

The difficulty is, of course, that the demand on schools to provide the bread-and-butter elements of education will not disappear as they move forward and face the challenges of an ever-changing world with constantly new demands. Schools, therefore, have not only to be creative in their own approaches to dealing with this, they must also be conscious of the need to provide opportunities for a varied educational experience for pupils – one that includes a creative view of work and life. An education that encourages creativity, innovation and enterprise will only work well if the school itself models these qualities within the way it operates. This has been recognized by central government as well as those who are operating in their own schools, and it will require a wholly new view of what education will look like and what its key purpose is.

> 'We will foster creativity and enterprise across our education and training system through radical new approaches to teaching and learning.' (DTI and DfES 2004)

2.3.4 Capacity – can we fill it?

It seems to be the case today that when an analysis is made of what makes a school effective, it is the outputs that are scrutinised. These, however, are the 'whats' and not the 'whys'. Outputs may involve obvious measures such as examination results, staff satisfaction, parental satisfaction, pupil satisfaction, teacher retention, and pupil (and teacher!) absence rates. All of these are fine in themselves, and they can of course be easily studied with quantifiable measures that are pleasing to the eye, particularly when plotted on graphs. But they don't necessarily tell us why these things are the way they are. As Hargreaves says: 'We need to understand the deeper cultural and structural underpinnings of schools that make them effective. I want to use concepts that explain why schools are successful and not merely describe the nature of the success.'

This is far more difficult, of course. It may be suggested that part of the problem is that we need to have a common language that describes what actually makes an effective school. This may not be as simple as it seems at first, and indeed we may not yet be at the position where this can be fully described. Hargreaves suggests, however, that:

'The quality of a school is explained in terms of three concepts – intellectual capital, social capital and organizational capital.'

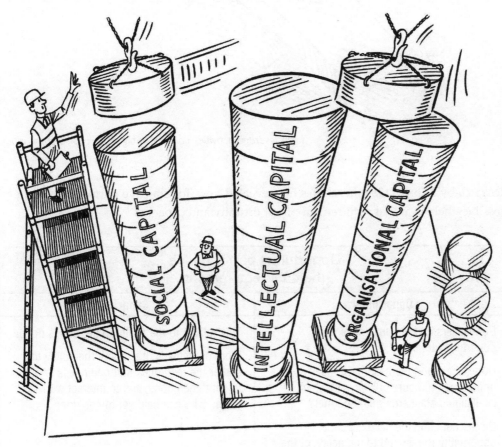

The three capitals of a school.

Professor Chris Day, in Book 3, Section five, refers to this. Essentially, the leader in a school has to try to build the capacity by means of the three 'capitals' that Hargreaves specifies. The school will then be in a state where best practice activities are constantly developed and strengthened. Hargreaves, again, says that the best practice activities that are of greatest interest are those that not only work but are of 'high leverage and easily transferable'. 'High leverage' refers to those activities that have great output impact in return for small input effort, and small input allocation in terms of human resources and finance.

High leverage activities can give a big output for a small input.

Research by Kanter (1989) in schools has revealed how, for effective performance to be possible, there is a dual requirement of opportunity and capacity.

Opportunity performance (the dual requirement)	
Opportunity	**Capacity**
Do teachers and the head have the opportunity to learn? Do teachers and the head have the opportunity to figure out ways in which challenging standards might be met? Do teachers and the head have the opportunity to respond to the needs of the children that they are responsible for?	This relates to the ability to get things done. More particularly, it is about the ability to gather the resources that one needs in order to get things done, and to interact with others who can help get things done.

Kanter warns that when opportunity and capacity are diminished, interest and excitement in one's work decreases. On the other hand, building on Kanter's framework, Milbrey McLaughlin and Sylvia Mei-Ling Yee (1988) found that enhanced levels of opportunity and capacity resulted in teachers experiencing greater stimulation at work and higher levels of motivation. In addition, they found that a teacher's effectiveness was directly related to the opportunities that teacher had –

▶ to develop basic competence

▶ to experience challenge in teaching

▶ to receive feedback about their importance

▶ to get support for trying new things

▶ to get support for their own growth.

Effective Leadership in Schools

Clearly a lot of this is directly linked to the continuing professional development (CPD) on offer to teachers in schools. Stoll in Stoll and Fink (2001) has made a direct link between what she refers to as capacity and the impact of teacher continuous professional development on this. She says that internal capacity is 'the power to engage in and sustain continuous learning of teachers and the school itself for the purpose of enhancing pupil learning'.

Stoll's research also showed that there was a clear association between capacity building and shared leadership. This all leads us to the conclusions we perhaps all suspected, which are that:

- effective schools depend on effective leaders

- effective leaders promote distributed or shared leadership in the schools

- these schools welcome and promote continual learning (CPD) for everyone

- the people in these schools value and care for all individuals

- the ethos of the school is one where the moral purpose and vision is shared by everyone

- with all these things in place there is a continual growth in capacity.

All elements are inextricably linked. Without one of these things the others will wither and die. Like an ecological system, they are mutually dependent on each other. There is a symbiotic relationship between the fundamental aspects of leadership and the character of the school they help to generate.

Leadership may, after all, be more about natural order and attaining harmony with the environment than we might previously have imagined.

Taking the leap

This section concerns the following:

2.4.1 Moving from being good to being great

▸ The challenge in education

2.4.2 Level 5 leadership

▸ Striving to reach the top

2.4.3 Ambition for the company

▸ – rather than for the leader

2.4.4 A compelling modesty

▸ Tell the truth.

2.4.5 Ferocious resolve

▸ – but resolve for the organization

2.4.6 The window and the mirror

▸ It's the view you take.

2.4.7 Cultivating Level 5 leadership

▸ What it takes.

2.4.1 Moving from being good to being great

In his book *Good to Great* Jim Collins (2002) raises a number of important issues about the characteristics of those leaders who have the capacity to take an organization from being 'good' to being 'great'. I think that what Collins indicates has real implications for a lot of the issues discussed in this book and the process and characteristics of leadership that will help to drive education forward. I feel, therefore, that it is worthwhile looking at some of the main conclusions about these 'Level 5' leaders.

As a background to this it is worth noting that Jim Collins worked with 21 research associates over a period of nearly five years, and that they examined over 1,400 Fortune 500 companies. Using a complex mix of qualitative and quantitative data, the results were synthesized to identify the 'drivers of good-to-great transformations'. The concepts were therefore developed by making empirical deductions directly from the data. They looked for the key concepts that enabled good-to-great companies to achieve nearly seven times the average stock market increase in 15 years. Good companies were doing well, but Jim Collins wanted to uncover what made certain companies take the leap to become great. His findings are as applicable to the world of education as they are for other businesses. Jim Collins' belief is that 'good is the enemy of great'. Collins indicates that this applies not just to companies but to all walks of life, and he makes the clear link with education when he opens the book by saying:

> *We don't have great schools, principally because we have good schools.*

People don't get round to doing great things because they settle for being good and having a good life. 'Why not?' many people will say. Well, I suppose the answer is that in education, if we truly want to move on to a new level, we have got to at least consider what this will entail.

What are the things we should be looking for in leaders that enable schools to move from being good to being great? Many of these qualities are discussed throughout VITAL 3. There are great schools out there in our system at the moment. The discussion in VITAL 3 will hopefully provide a mechanism for considering the key factors that enabled this to happen. So let's consider what Jim Collins tells us, and I think it is true to say that some of these things will surprise at least some people – as indeed they surprised Jim Collins and his team.

2.4.2 Level 5 leadership

Level 5 leadership is the kind of leadership that turned a good company into a great one. The diagram below represents the five levels of leadership.

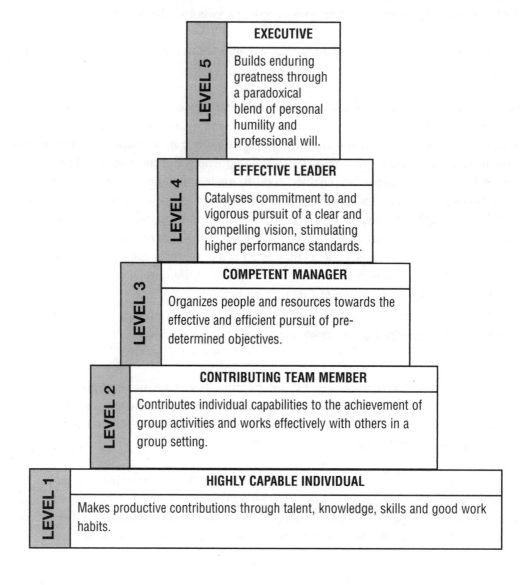

Level 5 leaders have certain fundamental characteristics. They have a blend of extreme personal humility and intense professional will. Level 5 leaders have incredible ambition, but their ambition is directed towards the needs of the organization and not themselves. They are not larger-than-life saviours with big personalities. Collins found that all the good-to-great companies had Level 5 leaders.

Collins gives specific examples of the Level 5 leaders encountered in the study. One of them is Colman Mockler of Gillette. Collins says about Mockler that 'his placid persona hid an inner intensity, a dedication to making anything he touched the best it could possibly be – not just because of what he would get, but because he simply couldn't imagine doing it any other way'. In the context of schools, and education in general, these sentiments certainly seem to strike a chord that we can all empathize with. Leadership in education should be about serving a bigger cause than the personal ambitions of the leaders themselves. The ambitions of the Level 5 leaders in the study were of a very different kind.

Effective Leadership in Schools

2.4.3 Ambition for the company

A critical quality of Level 5 leaders was that they had great ambition for the company rather than for individual riches and personal renown derived from their position in the company. They didn't seek to be the 'top dog', but rather wanted the success of the company to continue beyond their own period of tenure. To this end they would be looking for future success for the company exceeding what they themselves had experienced. They were constantly looking, therefore, for people to succeed them – and to succeed with success! By contrast, in three-quarters of the comparison companies who did not achieve greatness, leaders had set their successors up for failure, or chose weak successors, or both. Collins (2002) says:

> 'Level 5 leaders embody a paradoxical mix of personal humility and professional will. They are ambitious, to be sure, but ambitious first and foremost for the company, not themselves.'

It seems clear to me that we have a lot to learn from this in education. Schools are not always set up in such a way that succession is considered. Clearly part of the reason for this is the fire-fighting reactive situation that many leaders in schools find themselves in. There must be, as part of the structural fabric of schools, LEAs and all educational bodies, time built in for consideration of the primary needs and future direction and prosperity of the organization. Growing leaders in schools must be part of that thought process.

2.4.4 A compelling modesty

Collins says:

> '... in contrast to the very I-centric style of the comparison leaders, we were struck by how the good-to-great leaders didn't talk about themselves. During interviews with the good-to-great leaders, they'd talk about the company and the contributions of other executives as long as we'd like but would deflect discussion about their own contributions.'

The findings of the study were that these leaders were not displaying false modesty. People who worked with the Level 5 leaders used words like the following to describe them:

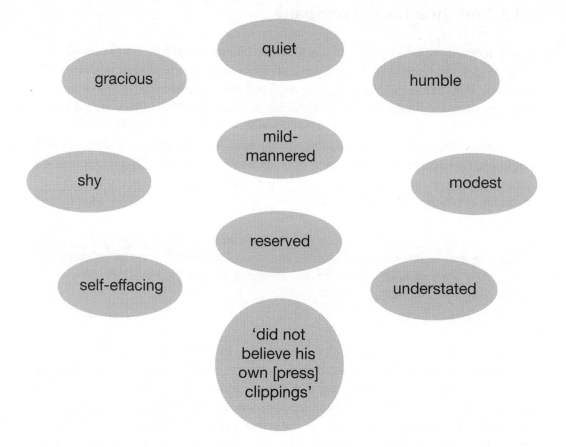

These are not exactly the words we would think of to describe the charismatic leader who has often been assumed to be necessary to 'sort things out' and turn an organization around. Indeed, they are not always the words that we would use to describe some of the leaders we may have encountered in schools at various times. Collins again:

'The good-to-great leaders never wanted to become larger-than-life heroes. They never aspired to be put on a pedestal or become unreachable icons. They were seemingly ordinary people quietly producing extraordinary results.'

In contrast, the comparison companies, in two-thirds of the cases, had a person with a 'gargantuan personal ego that contributed to the demise or continued mediocrity of the company'. Should this be taken into consideration in the way we appoint people into leadership positions in education, or are we very different? Fortunately the appointment of a charismatic leader to the position of headteacher in a 'failing school' is now somewhat discredited, but I wonder how many appointments to positions of leadership are made on the basis of characteristics that are in any way comparable with those noted above. I have certainly not seen them explicitly mentioned in job adverts in the *Times Educational Supplement* alongside the more obvious statements about 'drive, energy and vision', for example. Maybe it is just too bold a move for anyone to take, and for anyone to believe that these characteristics are being explicitly sought. Perhaps somebody should make, maybe somebody already has made, the first move on this.

Effective Leadership in Schools

2.4.5 Ferocious resolve

The leaders of the good-to-great companies also exhibited an unwavering resolve to do whatever needed to be done to make the company great. They are fanatically driven, with a stoic determination to do almost anything to make the company great. Nepotism was not allowed, and certainly not if this meant that the company was not successful. Another interesting feature is that the good-to-great leaders were more often than not nurtured within the organization. They were not outside leaders who were brought in to shake things up. So much so, in fact, that 10 out of 11 of the good-to-great CEOs came from inside the company.

Again, this is useful to consider in relation to what is often perceived to be needed in schools. Rather than a revolution, it is often an evolution that is needed, and not to believe that there is anyone inside the school who can take on the critical role of leader is surely to be blind to the talents that exist within a school – or, alternatively, an indicator of poor leadership in terms of not nurturing leaders within the school.

2.4.6 The window and the mirror

Collins (2002) reports that the Level 5 leaders refer to 'luck' on a consistent basis. This emphasis on luck, Collins adds, was 'part of a pattern that we came to call the window and the mirror'. In a nutshell, what Collins is observing with regard to the Level 5 leaders is the fact that they 'look out of the window to apportion credit to factors outside themselves when things go well (and if they cannot find a specific person or event to give credit to, they credit luck). At the same time, they look in the mirror to apportion responsibility, never blaming bad luck when things go poorly.'

Just for good measure, the comparison leaders did just the opposite. I am sure you can fill in the details of how this appeared for yourself: we have all heard people blame 'bad luck' or other people when things go badly, and attempt to take credit without thanking other people when things go well. This was not what Collins found that Level 5 leaders did.

Leadership is about the mirror and the window.

2.4.7 Cultivating Level 5 leadership

A critical question for us in education is whether we can grow people who will become Level 5 leaders. It is sobering to realize that of the 1,435 companies that Collins originally looked at, only 11 made the very 'tough cut' into the study. It is Collins' view that there are some people who can and some who can't. Those who can't are people who are not able to 'subjugate their egotistical needs to building something larger and more lasting than themselves'. Collins says that these people will desire fame, fortune, adulation and power from their work over and above what they build, create and contribute towards. The question is, are such people often those who make it into key positions in businesses and indeed education? Collins believes that the larger group of people are those who are able to evolve into Level 5 leaders. Their intrinsic nature, together with the right circumstances, or nurture, will enable them to develop into Level 5 leaders. The 'right circumstances' may be thought about and actively sought, or may be part of the fortune of their lives. Therefore, such things as:

- self-reflection

- conscious personal development

- an appropriate mentor

- loving parents

- a significant life experience

can all contribute towards an individual becoming a Level 5 leader.

The great thing here for many of us is that some of these things are within our control. Perhaps the only element in the above which is outside our control is whether we are blessed to have had loving parents. The rest, it can be argued, are things we can influence in some way and to some degree. The problem, Collins says, is not that there is a dearth of potential Level 5 leaders; in fact, that they exist all around us. The difficulty is in finding them, and Collins suggests that we should seek them out wherever there are extraordinary results taking place but where no individual 'steps forward to claim excess credit'.

The conclusion is that there are many people around who can become Level 5 leaders but there are not many of them in the top leadership positions. It would be unwise to assume that this is does not apply to education as much as it is does to the businesses Collins looked at. It is a challenge for all of us in education to fully consider this if we wish to make the substantial improvements in life opportunities that we all want for all of the young people in this country.

'We don't have great schools, principally because we have good schools.'

Jim Collins

Continuing professional development

This section concerns the following:

2.5.1 CPD – as important as teaching and learning

▸ Strengthening teaching and learning requires CPD.

2.5.2 What is CPD?

▸ A look at some of the definitions

2.5.3 The impact of CPD

▸ The EPPI review findings

2.5.1 CPD – as important as teaching and learning

Trends come and go. The priorities of today seem to be lost or forgotten tomorrow. There is a great emphasis on teaching and learning in schools at the moment – almost as if this was something that schools were not interested in before! Teaching and learning has always been there and central to most schools, but perhaps only in the past few years has it been talked about, and encouragement given for it to be talked about, as the core business of schools. Maybe people just took it for granted that this is what we are all about in schools. On the other hand, if it is not explicitly discussed, then it is possible to lose sight of this core purpose amid the hurly-burly of everyday school life, with reactive priorities, as well as demands that are constantly becoming new priorities, putting new pressures on the school. It is right, therefore, always to put the development of effective teaching and learning, and the provision of opportunities for every individual in the school to flourish, at the top of the school agenda. This, as already discussed, is part of a moral purpose.

Another aspect of school life that we should constantly talk about is continuing professional development (CPD). If we want to provide the pupils in our schools with the very best education we can give, we must never ignore the chief way in which that will be achieved, namely by the continuing development of the teachers and all those who work in our schools. Developing the people who compose our school workforce should become a core purpose, complementing the pursuit of excellence in teaching and learning. Without paying attention to the former, the latter will not happen.

Equally at the top of the agenda should be the provision of CPD for teachers, support staff, and indeed, everyone associated with the school. A school should therefore plan, coordinate and review the way in which it provides a lifelong learning environment for everyone – beginning, perhaps, with teachers and extending to classroom assistants, all support staff, governors and parents. To these groups you could add others, such as local (and not so local) business people, higher education institutions and colleges of further education. Is this going too far? Well, for some it may not be the first step, but it should surely follow close behind on the track forged by work developed for teachers. In this way the organization can become a learning school.

CPD, in my view, therefore, is a core priority alongside teaching and learning. The two are inextricably linked, and a dual focus on both is needed. Effective systemic change can only take place alongside a clearly defined role for professional development. There has been a movement away from CPD as 'individuals going away on courses', and the main reason for this (and the reason why it has often failed in the past), as Fullan explains, is the difficulty of changed individuals coming back to a system that is still the same. The changed individuals may not have the capacity to impact on the school they return to, owing to lack of authority, or a system that does not encourage their involvement in development and change. Working on CPD within the school, rather than going out on courses, is therefore often regarded now as more effective in terms of the impact it can have on the process of change. External courses and external expertise can still provide teachers (and others involved with schools) with important ways of adapting and developing their practice if, as well as providing new information and skills, they address ways of changing the context within a school so as to accommodate these. Fullan (2001) says:

> 'Incidentally, focusing on information rather than use is why sending individuals and even teams to external training by itself does not work. Leading in a culture of change does not mean placing changed individuals into unchanged environments. Rather, change leaders work on changing the context, helping create new settings conducive to learning and sharing their learning.'

Day et al. add that the literature suggests 'that ongoing success, then, in self-managing schools will depend upon the commitment and abilities of headteachers to promote professional development awareness cultures in their schools' (Day et al. 2003). Day adds that the work of Ruddock (1991) indicates that:

> 'Teachers who are provided regularly and appropriately with opportunities for self-renewal of vision and purpose, and who are helped to acquire new habits and review existing habits of thought, disposition and practice, will, it seems, develop their capacity to contribute to the task of enhancing the quality of students' learning opportunities and to the development of their colleagues' thinking practices.'

Emphasizing the importance of CPD to pupil progress, Stoll (in Stoll and Fink 2001) quotes Barth (1990), who says:

> 'Probably nothing in a school has more impact on students in terms of skills development, self-confidence, or classroom behaviour than the personal and professional growth of their teachers.'

An additional importance of CPD for teachers is that it provides a model of lifelong learning, which pupils will see as well as hear about within the school. According to Seymour Sarason's model (1990, quoted in Sergiovanni 2002):

> 'It is virtually impossible to create and sustain over time conditions for productive learning for students when they do not exist for teachers.'

Effective schools realize that CPD is essential within the structure of the school. Effective CPD is needed to advance the school, to make it a place where innovation, creativity and risk-taking are all promoted. Effective CPD is linked with performance management and school improvement in such a way that it contributes to the development of the individual and the school simultaneously. CPD is important because it:

▶ makes staff versatile

▶ improves pupils' learning

▶ creates vibrant learning communities

▶ helps to recruit and maintain staff

- ▸ broadens horizons
- ▸ keeps schools thinking about the future and opportunities that exist.

Leadership of CPD, therefore, is critical to the advancement of education in our schools.

CPD – five levels

To advance education we must pay regard to CPD at five levels: the national, the regional, the LEA, the school and the individual. Each of these is critically important and requires challenging leadership skills, together with acceptance of ownership (by individuals, that is, teachers, support staff, LEA officials, DfES personnel – as well as by the collective whole).

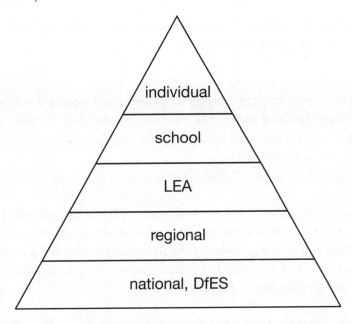

Some schools may question spending time and energy on the professional development of their staff. Ultimately these schools will find that they are likely to lose their best teachers and to fail to develop as a school that is vibrant and welcomes new and invigorating ideas that benefit everyone.

I would argue that the benefits of CPD are clear and, as Early and Bubb (2004) have stated, that CPD:

- ▸ 'helps everyone to be more effective in their jobs, so pupils learn and behave better and achieve higher standards;
- ▸ improves retention and recruitment – word gets around about the places where you are looked after, and where you are not;
- ▸ contributes to a positive ethos where people feel valued and motivated;
- ▸ makes for a learning community – the pupils are learning and so are the staff;
- ▸ is a professional responsibility and entitlement;
- ▸ saves money – the cost of recruiting and inducting a new teacher into a school can be about £4,000.'

These points explain why it is vital to treat management and leadership of the precious resource of staff in schools, and their continuing professional development, as key priorities alongside teaching and learning.

We all want to raise the profile of teaching and education, bringing about the perception of teaching as a true profession where progress and development are valued. A true profession is one where it is expected that people will continually learn and develop throughout their careers. Leaders in education today must never lose sight of the importance of CPD in shaping the future of the profession.

2.5.2 What is CPD?

CPD is all the formal and informal training and learning that enables individuals to improve their own practice. Bolam (1993) defines it as:

> 'any professional development activities engaged in by teachers which enhance their knowledge and skills and enable them to consider their attitudes and approaches to the education of children, with a view to improving the quality of the teaching and learning process.'

I would extend this to include everyone involved in schools who ultimately impacts on the education of children. Bolam's definition highlights the strong relationship between CPD and teaching and learning, and why the two must be considered together. Chris Day, a contributor to Book 3 of VITAL 3, explains how CPD goes beyond the acquisition of knowledge and teaching skills. He says:

> 'Professional development consists of all natural learning experiences and those conscious and planned activities that are intended to be of direct or indirect benefit to the individual, group or school and which contribute, through these, to the quality of education in the classroom. It is the process by which, alone and with others, teachers review, renew and extend their commitment as change agents to the moral purposes of teaching; and by which they acquire and develop critically the knowledge, skills and emotional intelligence essential to good professional thinking, planning and practice with children, young people and colleagues through each phase of their teaching lives.' (Day 1999)

In 2001 the DfES launched its strategy for CPD and stated that:

> 'By professional development we mean any activity that increases the skills, knowledge or understanding of teachers, and their effectiveness in schools.'

An understanding of CPD has to include the idea that staff in schools will learn best where there is a collaborative ethos within a 'learning-organization' environment. A rich mix of continuous learning, experimentation, action research, risk-taking, valuing of expertise and a willingness to test out ideas (both internally and externally generated) is the model of CPD that will bring about sustainable change and improved standards. CPD needs to be taken seriously by all of us. Early and Bubb (2004) say:

> 'There are two groups of learner within schools – young people and adults – and we neglect either at our peril. If teachers and other staff are not seen as continuous learners by the school itself, how can young adults engage youngsters in any meaningful pursuit of learning?'

CPD is the glue that bonds all effective aspects of a school together.

2.5.3 The impact of CPD

In order to uncover the impact of CPD it is interesting to look at the findings of a review of CPD literature published in June 2003. This was called an 'EPPI' review. (The EPPI-Centre is the Evidence for Policy and Practice Information and Co-ordinating Centre, which is part of the Social Science Research Unit (SSRU) at the Institute of Education, University of London.) The aim was to systematically review the literature on CPD in order to discover evidence about sustained, collaborative CPD and its effect on teaching and learning. For the purposes of the review, collaborative CPD involved teachers working together, which could be teachers working with an LEA, with an HEI, or with other professional colleagues on a sustained basis.

The report examines how the impact of CPD was realized and manifested. First of all, looking at this in relation to teachers, the changes in teacher behaviours reported in the studies included:

▸ greater confidence among the teachers

▸ enhanced beliefs among teachers about their power to make a difference to their pupils' learning (self-efficacy)

▸ developing enthusiasm for collaborative working, notwithstanding initial anxieties about being observed and receiving feedback

▸ greater commitment to changing practice and willingness to try new things.

Confidence, beliefs, enthusiasm and commitment – these all seem to be pretty powerful things that collaborative CPD is impacting on.

For full benefit from the changes that CPD can bring, clearly commitment is needed on the part of leaders. The report indicates that the positive outcomes of the impact of collaborative CPD sometimes emerged only after periods of relative discomfort in trying out new approaches, and that things often got worse before they got better. Throughout the process, however, collaboration was important in sustaining change. The time for discussion, planning and feedback, and access to suitable resources, were a common concern in many of the studies, and leaders in schools will need to be aware of this when they plan for collaborative CPD in their schools.

The report also describes how the impact of CPD was realized and manifested in terms of benefits for students. The outcomes for students were focused on measured improvements in student performance or specifically assessed learning approaches, including:

▸ demonstrable enhancement of student motivation

▸ improvements in performance, such as improved test results, greater ability in decoding, and enhanced reading fluency

▸ more positive responses to specific subjects

▸ better organization of work

▸ increased sophistication in response to questions.

Positive impacts on students, including motivation, performance, responses, and organization of their work, are powerful stimuli to encourage collaborative CPD among teachers. Other benefits in terms of student attitudes and beliefs included increased satisfaction with their work, enhanced motivation, increased confidence and increasingly active participation.

There was also some evidence that where CPD aimed to increase collaborative working among pupils, the collaboration among teacher participants acted as a model.

The EPPI findings relate to collaborative CPD, but it is likely that many of the benefits noted are an intrinsic part of many CPD activities.

BIBLIOGRAPHY

Barth R. (1990) *Improving Schools from Within. Parents and principals can make a difference.* San Francisco: Jossey-Bass.

Bennis W. (2003) *On Becoming a Leader.* USA: perseus Publishing

Bolam R. (1993) *Recent Developments and Emerging Issues in the Continuing Professional Development of Teachers.* London: GTC.

Collins J. (2002) *Good to Great.* London: Random House.

Day C. (1999) *Developing Teachers: The challenge of lifelong learning.* London: Falmer.

Day C., Harris A., Hadfield M., Tolley H. and Beresford J. (2003) *Leading Schools in Times of Change.* Maidenhead: Open University Press.

DfES (2001):

> ▸ *Good Value CPD.* Prolog ref. no: 0059/2001.
>
> ▸ *Learning and Teaching.* Prolog ref. no: 0071/2001.
>
> ▸ *Helping You Develop. Guidance on Producing a Professional Development Record.* Prolog ref no: 0649/2001.
>
> ▸ *Teachers' Standards Framework.* Prolog ref no: 0647/2001.

DTI/DfEE (2004) *A White Paper on Enterprise, Skills and Innovation.* http://www.dti.gov.uk/opportunityforall

Early P. and Bubb S. (2004) *Leading and Managing Continuing Professional Development.* London: Paul Chapman Publishing.

EPPI-Centre (2003) *How does collaborative Continuing Professional Development (CPD) for teachers of the 5-16 age range affect teaching and learning?* http://eppi.ioe.ac.uk/EPPIweb/home.aspx

Fullan M. (2001) *Leading in a Culture of Change.* San Francisco: Jossey-Bass.

Hargreaves D. H. (2003) *Education Epidemic.* London: Demos.

Hesselbein F., Goldsmith M. and Beckhard R. (eds) (1996) *The Leader of the Future.* New York: Jossey-Bass.

Kakabadse A., Nortier F. and Abramovici N.-B. (1998) *Success in Sight: Visioning.* London: International Thomson Business Press.

Kanter R. M. (1989) *When Giants Learn to Dance.* New York: Simon & Schuster.

MacBeath J. and Mortimore P. (2001) *Improving School Effectiveness.* Maidenhead: Open University Press.

McLaughlin M. and Mei-Ling Yee S. (1988). *School as a Place to Have a Career. Building of professional cultures in schools.* New York: Teacher College Press.

Ruddock J. (1991) *Innovation and Change: Developing involvement and understanding.* Buckingham: Open University Press.

Sarason S. B. (1990) *The Predictable Failure of Educational Reform.* San Francisco: Jossey Bass

Sergiovanni T. J. (2002) *Leadership. What's in it for schools?* London: RoutledgeFalmer.

Stoll L. and Fink D. (2001) *Changing Our Schools*. Maidenhead: Open University Press.

Swainston T. (2002) *Effective Teachers: A reflective resource for enhancing practice*. Stafford: Network Educational Press.

Swainston T. (2003) *Effective Teachers in Primary Schools: A reflective resource for enhancing practice*. Stafford: Network Educational Press.

UNESCO (1996) *Learning: The Treasure Within*. UNESCO report for Education for the 21st Century, published by the German UNESCO Commission. Neuwied; Kriftel; Berlin: Luchterhand.

Watkins C., Carnell E., Lodge C. and Whalley C. (1996) *Effective Learning*. School Improvement Network Research Matters No. 5. London: Institute of Education.

Index

Other titles from Network Educational Press

ACCELERATED LEARNING SERIES
Accelerated Learning: A User's Guide
     by Alistair Smith, Mark Lovatt & Derek Wise
Accelerated Learning in the Classroom by Alistair Smith
Accelerated Learning in Practice by Alistair Smith
The ALPS Approach: Accelerated Learning in Primary Schools
     by Alistair Smith & Nicola Call
The ALPS Approach Resource Book by Alistair Smith & Nicola Call
ALPS StoryMaker by Stephen Bowkett
MapWise by Oliver Caviglioli & Ian Harris
Creating an Accelerated Learning School by Mark Lovatt & Derek Wise
Thinking for Learning by Mel Rockett & Simon Percival
Reaching out to all learners by Cheshire LEA
Move It: Physical movement and learning by Alistair Smith
Coaching Solutions by Will Thomas & Alistair Smith

ABLE AND TALENTED CHILDREN COLLECTION
Effective Provision for Able and Talented Children by Barry Teare
Effective Resources for Able and Talented Children by Barry Teare
More Effective Resources for Able and Talented Children by Barry Teare
Challenging Resources for Able and Talented Children by Barry Teare
Enrichment Activities for Able and Talented Children by Barry Teare
Parents' and Carers' Guide for Able and Talented Children by Barry Teare

LEARNING TO LEARN
Let's Learn How to Learn: Workshops for Key Stage 2 by UFA National Team
Brain Friendly Revision by UFA National Team
Creating a Learning to Learn School by Toby Greany & Jill Rodd
Teaching Pupils How to Learn by Bill Lucas, Toby Greany, Jill Rodd & Ray Wicks

PRIMARY RESOURCES
*Promoting Children's Well-Being in the Primary Years: The Right from
    the Start Handbook edited* by Andrew Burrell and Jeni Riley
But Why? Developing philosophical thinking in the classroom
    by Sara Stanley with Steve Bowkett
Foundations of Literacy by Sue Palmer & Ros Bayley
Help Your Child To Succeed by Bill Lucas & Alistair Smith
Help Your Child To Succeed – Toolkit by Bill Lucas & Alistair Smith
That's English! by Tim Harding
That's Maths! by Tim Harding
That's Science! by Tim Harding
The Thinking Child by Nicola Call with Sally Featherstone

The Thinking Child Resource Book by Nicola Call with Sally Featherstone
Numeracy Activities Key Stage 2 by Afzal Ahmed & Honor Williams
Numeracy Activities Key Stage 3 by Afzal Ahmed, Honor Williams
       & George Wickham

EXCITING ICT

New Tools for Learning: Accelerated Learning meets ICT by John Davitt
Exciting ICT in Maths by Alison Clark-Jeavons
Exciting ICT in English by Tony Archdeacon
Exciting ICT in History by Ben Walsh

CREATIVE THINKING

Think it–Map it! by Ian Harris & Oliver Caviglioli
Thinking Skills & Eye Q by Oliver Caviglioli, Ian Harris & Bill Tindall
Reaching out to all thinkers by Ian Harris & Oliver Caviglioli
With Drama in Mind by Patrice Baldwin
Imagine That... by Stephen Bowkett
Self-Intelligence by Stephen Bowkett
StoryMaker Catch Pack by Stephen Bowkett

EFFECTIVE LEARNING & LEADERSHIP

Effective Heads of Department by Phil Jones & Nick Sparks
Leading the Learning School by Colin Weatherley
Closing the Learning Gap by Mike Hughes
Strategies for Closing the Learning Gap by Mike Hughes with Andy Vass
Transforming Teaching & Learning
       by Colin Weatherley with Bruce Bonney, John Kerr & Jo Morrison
Effective Learning Activities by Chris Dickinson
Tweak to Transform by Mike Hughes
Making Pupil Data Powerful by Maggie Pringle & Tony Cobb
Raising Boys' Achievement by Jon Pickering
Effective Teachers by Tony Swainston
Effective Teachers in Primary Schools by Tony Swainston

EFFECTIVE PERSONNEL MANAGEMENT

The Well Teacher – management strategies for beating stress, promoting staff health & reducing absence by Maureen Cooper
Managing Challenging People – dealing with staff conduct
   by Maureen Cooper & Bev Curtis
Managing Poor Performance – handling staff capability issues
   by Maureen Cooper & Bev Curtis
Managing Recruitment and Selection – appointing the best staff
   by Maureen Cooper & Bev Curtis
Managing Allegations Against Staff – personnel and child protection issues in schools by Maureen Cooper & Bev Curtis

Managing Redundancies – dealing with reduction and reorganisation of staff by Maureen Cooper & Bev Curtis

Paying Staff in Schools – performance management and pay in schools by Bev Curtis

VISIONS OF EDUCATION SERIES

Discover Your Hidden Talents: The essential guide to lifelong learning by Bill Lucas

The Power of Diversity by Barbara Prashnig

The Brain's Behind It by Alistair Smith

Wise Up by Guy Claxton

The Unfinished Revolution by John Abbott & Terry Ryan

The Learning Revolution by Gordon Dryden & Jeannette Vos

EMOTIONAL INTELLIGENCE

Becoming Emotionally Intelligent by Catherine Corrie

Lend Us Your Ears by Rosemary Sage

Class Talk by Rosemary Sage

A World of Difference by Rosemary Sage

Best behaviour and Best behaviour FIRST AID by Peter Relf, Rod Hirst, Jan Richardson & Georgina Youdell

Best behaviour FIRST AID also available separately

DISPLAY MATERIAL

Move It posters: Physical movement and learning by Alistair Smith

Bright Sparks by Alistair Smith

More Bright Sparks by Alistair Smith

Leading Learning by Alistair Smith

NEWLY QUALIFIED TEACHERS

Lessons are for Learning by Mike Hughes

Classroom Management by Philip Waterhouse & Chris Dickinson

Getting Started by Henry Liebling

SCHOOL GOVERNORS

Questions School Governors Ask by Joan Sallis

Basics for School Governors by Joan Sallis

The Effective School Governor by David Marriott (including audio tape)

For more information and ordering details, please consult our website
www.networkpress.co.uk